THE PATH TO HEARING ANGELS & GUIDES

THE PATH TO HEARING ANGELS & GUIDES

21 Days of Meditation

DEBBRA LUPIEN

Lupien Limited

Lupien Limited

Cresco, PA 18326

Cover image by Tim Hill from Pixabay

Metatron's Cube by Nicolás Damián Visceglio from Pixabay

Voice of the Akashic Records, Book 2

The Path to Hearing Angels & Guides/ Debbra Lupien — 1st ed.

Library of Congress Control Number: 2021922470

ISBN 978-0-9994880-3-4 (Kindle)

ISBN 978-0-9994880-4-1 (Paperback)

CONTENTS

Reader Bonus

Get your **Reader Bonus**: an ebook containing nine additional channeled messages from Archangel Metatron for your post-challenge enrichment. Plus an invitation to my private challenge group where you'll find guideposts for the challenge, along with encouragement and support to ensure your success and spiritual growth. https://akashaunleashed.com/lightworkers-path

To the Lightworkers of the World, my fellow sojourners on the ascension path: Thank you for your steadfast commitment and perseverance as we join together to make this world a better place for ourselves and for the generations to come.

A Note From The Author

This book sprang from my experience of doing the 21-Day Meditation challenge as requested by Archangel Metatron.

Each day I faithfully recorded my experience so that I wouldn't forget any details. It was only after my challenge was complete that I realized Metatron intended these daily messages to be compiled as a guidebook (available separately) to help enhance the experience and facilitate the journey to greater peace and self awareness.

Through your effort, you will gain a deeper understanding of yourself, and a stronger, more fluid connection with your Akashic team. This is the easy peasy key to hearing your angels and guides. It's one part trust, one part confidence, and one part toning your *hearing* muscle. Each experience builds upon the last until you find connecting with your Akashic team is *almost* as easy and natural as breathing. Almost...

My recommendation is that you read this book in its entirety in order to more fully understand the scope, and dare I say *rules*, of the challenge.

Afterwards, having seen the big picture, select a date to begin your own challenge. As you begin each day, you may find it useful to review the corresponding chapter (day) to bolster your confidence.

This is *your* journey, so feel free to do it in the way that feels best for you. Leaning into your intuition and making the most empowered choice is the basis of your soul journey.

Of course if you discover somewhere during the initial read that you don't want to wait, then go ahead and start. The most important rule is to do this in the way that works best for you ensuring you'll successfully complete all 21 days.

I highly recommend you join the special Facebook group I created to support you through this challenge journey, as well as to share experiences with others. That will greatly enhance the experience and accelerate your ascension journey.

I look forward to meeting you and hearing about your journey in the group.

Debbra

P.S. You can access all the links referenced in these chapters on page 133, the *Connecting* page.

METATRON HAS ALSO PROVIDED A COMPANION workbook containing daily messages, which function as guideposts to encourage and help you stay on track during your meditation challenge journey. You can find it on Amazon or through the links on page 133.

Prologue: The Assignment

December 13, 2020 was one of those rare times I actually sat down to meditate.

Immediately my mind wandered to thinking about a very long To Do List. Then I started hearing *The Name Game* song, a silly ditty supplied by my guides to help me refocus.

Their tactic worked, because in just moments a message started broadcasting that would prove to be of great consequence to the light workers of the world.

For quite some time Archangel Metatron has been transmitting prophetic messages about the future of Earth and her inhabitants. The message on this day speaks to that prophecy: *The end of bigotry and hate on Earth.*

As Earth and her inhabitants shift into a higher vibrational frequency, we will evolve into a new golden age of love and peace.

METATRON: WHEN FACED WITH HATRED YOU MAY join the haters, or you may choose to notice the contrast and focus your efforts on staying in the energetic space of love.

Sometimes one must be confronted with a thing in order to understand the thing. This present hatred is so visceral it can be mistaken for nothing else. Therefore, the choice is made more stark. You must take a side or be swept away in the roiling energetic waters between.

The time for standing back and silently observing is past. This is your moment. Raise your voice for love and peace or be trampled by the masses who have chosen hatred and turmoil.

This *is* the epic battle between lightness and dark. There's no in between.

Fear not for you are fortified with the power of legions of angels. They stand even now at the ready to join you in bringing about a new golden era of peace and love. Your utopia. But it will not be attained by indifference, rather it requires commitment and dedication to the cause.

Do you desire this promised golden age enough to do whatever it takes to bring it about? What if it means sacrificing your life's blood? What if it means standing against those whom you love? What are you willing to sacrifice to bring about the return of *The Light*.

This is your Biblical moment. Take a stand or stand for nothing.

Debbra: At this point I was getting distracted, wondering whether my translation was correct.

Metatron: Are you Debbra willing to sit here as long as it takes to properly translate this message?

Debbra: Yes, it is my mission to share your message. Bring it on. We are so ready to hear.

After a mere two minutes my thoughts began to wander to all the tasks awaiting me, some time sensitive. How long is this going to take?

If I can't last even two minutes am I really ready? What could be more important than restoring love and peace to the planet?

Metatron: It would be wise to commit to at least 15 minutes per day of meditation. That is enough to tone the muscle, discipline the mind, and to achieve greater focus with ease. This process is about allowing, not struggling.

Simply sit quietly and allow the messages to flow. Do not judge what you receive. For even if it be less than perfect, it is good enough and will get better with practice. It is when you hold yourself to such high standards that you snatch victory from the jaws of defeat.

Simply allow as if you are floating on a peaceful pond where the water gently supports you. Trust that you will not sink. Trust that the sun will shine upon and warm you while you remain thus situated.

Trust and remain in this gentle, safe space for as long as is required to complete the transmission. Yes your skin may be a bit wrinkly after an extended time in the water, but that is temporary. Soon enough it will shift back to a normal state of being, just as shall you.

Until now it has been less important that you commit to regular meditation, however, now that the battle is at hand, it is vital as this is the way you maintain your protective energy shield. It must be maintained so that it will withstand the negative energy bursts to come — and there will be many.

Debbra: A vision comes of thousands of lightworkers sitting quietly in their personal space meditating. Their collective energy forms a dome-like shield that, when fully powered, will be impenetrable by the forces of darkness. Does that mean if we don't practice enough our shield will fail?

Metatron: Yes. This is your planet, your lives and if you aren't willing to stand up and defend the way of the light, darkness will prevail — at least temporarily. There will be other lives and other chances, but why postpone the inevitable? Sooner or later you *must* cross this bridge and undergo this rite of passage.

You must commit yourself to the cause of love and light and then you will prevail. You've already been guaranteed success, if you put in the effort. The deck is stacked in your favor. Which side are you on?

Once you make up your mind and take up your place in the battle, victory will come quickly. What's required is a large enough body of energy to create an impenetrable shield. Darkness will quickly retreat to another time and place where it will once more take up arms against the light. But that is none of your concern. There are bigger battles yet to be fought. Right now your focus is upon saving yourselves and the planet so that you have the opportunity to bask in the new golden age.

The past is gone, the future is not yet determined. Put your focus upon the here and now, which is where your power presently lies.

Yes there is much sorrow at loss of life, and for some home and hearth, but this is fleeting.

Reach out to one another, form a united front against the darkness and you *will* transform yourselves and the world.

Imagine a world devoid of bigotry and hate. A world where neighbors help neighbors, where everyone loves and respects the planet. Energy and manifestations flow like breath before the advent of Covid. Disease dissipates because it cannot exist in a state of balanced energy, aligned with soul.

We can hear you scoffing that this is too good to be true. It might be if you choose to make that your reality.

Your earth reality can split with one experiencing the golden age of peace and love and one facing death and destruction. Which side are you on?

Debbra: With that the message ended, leaving me pondering how best to share this challenge with other awakening souls.

When to begin? What format would be best?

I need time to plan…

Metatron: Not if you listen to guidance and set it up properly. That's an egoic excuse to delay.

Debbra: Do I need to create meditations? What is the best structure? How do I organize so people don't get bored?

Metatron: Don't worry about boredom. Better boredom than too much variety.

Debbra: I began the challenge the next day, recording my experience on each of the 21 days.

There were many bumps along the way, but it was so worth hanging in to completion.

After you've read my *imperfect* daily experience, I hope you'll be eager to start your own challenge.

As Metatron said, it's not about perfection, it's about commitment and discipline on your ascension journey.

It's about preparing to win the epic battle of lightworkers vs. the darkness of bigotry and hate.

Introduction

As a spiritual teacher I sometimes meditate to channel a particular message (when feeling led), or to get answers to questions. However, until recently I didn't have a regular practice.

Shocking, right? Most people assume that being the Voice of the Akashic Records requires copious amounts of meditation. Nope. Even though I feel I should meditate regularly I simply haven't made it a priority because, you know… life.

That is until December of 2020 when Archangel Metatron stepped up the game with an assignment to meditate fifteen minutes per day for 21 days.

Piece of cake, I thought. I can enter a meditative state in seconds. I grew excited imagining all sorts of wonderful new insights being shared during each session.

Except, that's not quite how it turned out…

The Rules of the Game

Yes game, because when you approach meditation with playfulness, the experience will be richer, deeper, and more meaningful.

Meditation will change your life — if you let it.

That's a pretty big claim, but if you'll stick with me, I promise to present a convincing case and perhaps you'll find yourself committing to your own regular meditation practice.

If you're someone who believes you *can't* meditate or that you're required to sit in the lotus position chanting *OM*, you'd be wrong on both counts.

Everyone *can* meditate once they understand a few basic principles.

- *All you need is a block of time, and a comfortable, quiet space*

- *Make a commitment to yourself and follow through*

- *Be as consistent as possible*

- *Allow the experience to organically unfold*

- *Refrain from judging yourself and the experience*

In the pages that follow I've documented my experience each day, including the days when life interfered. Yep, I missed some days along the way, but did eventually complete the assignment. In the end it was so incredibly worth it.

It was with you in mind, Dear Reader, that I carefully documented the mind games that often derailed my meditations. They can happen to anyone — no matter how practiced. There will simply be times when your focus is scattered and you're unable to corral errant thoughts. *This is normal.*

The remedy is to honor your commitment and keep showing up. Time spent in this intentional way is an investment in yourself and the payoff is immeasurable.

Your guides are always on standby: ready, willing and able to connect. *You* are the missing link. But that can all change with commitment, determination and practice. That's what this challenge is all about.

Ready when you are...

Pre-Meditation Preparation

You may choose to set an alarm for a specific amount of time or you may just flow with whatever time feels right. Either is fine. This is about you finding the best path for yourself.

Method 1

Begin by connecting with your Akashic Records using the *Akasha Unleashed Access Prayer* (end of chapter), or use whatever means you feel comfortable with. By intentionally connecting with your Records *before* meditating, you can trust that what you're receiving is only truth, love, and light, for your highest good.

At the beginning of a meditation many nonsensical things may run through your mind like a hamster on a wheel. That's ok, just take another deep breath and pay attention to your breathing. Don't stress about errant thoughts.

State out loud the thing you want to focus on. Feel the vibration of the words on your tongue. Allow the words to reverberate through your brain. Let this be a multi-sensory experience.

If your thoughts bounce around a bit that's ok.

No stress, no strain, that's counterproductive. Just as you would with a distracted child, keep gently bringing your thoughts back to your breathing and/or what you want to focus upon.

However, don't be rigid. If your thoughts stray to something even better, allow them to explore for a bit and see where they go. This very well could be the opening your team was looking for to communicate something of import.

Even if your entire meditation is spent deep breathing and refocusing that's fine. You're finding your way along a new path — the path to enlightenment — where hearing your angels and guides with ease is almost as natural as breathing. Isn't that worth some effort?

When your time has elapsed, thank your guides with a grateful heart and go on about your day.

Continue this process daily, if possible, or at least a few times a week. Soon you'll find that you're able to quickly slip into a relaxed/receiving state.

Method 2

Begin with the *Akasha Unleashed Access Prayer*. Then use a recorded, guided visualization that resonates with you. When you reach the end of the recording, linger in that relaxed, open space connected to your guides.

In the beginning allow whatever wants to come through to do so. (Having begun with the Access Prayer, you can trust what you receive is from your Akashic Records.) Later on as you become more fluent in your practice, you'll be able to enjoy a two-way dialog. Just remember you have to walk before you run. Be patient with yourself.

Toning The Muscle

Over time you may start to notice more activity during meditations in the form of physical sensations, visuals, sounds, or a sort of seeing/feeling words appear in your brain. Almost like a banner or movie screen. This experience is individual so whatever you experience is perfect for you.

With continued practice, the day will come when you're able to hear your angels and guides while simply going about your day. You will marvel at how frequently they interact, sharing wisdom, inspiration, and marvelous synchronicities. Daily life feels downright magical. Your soul sings with joy and gratitude.

Expanding Your Experience

Meditating is often like daydreaming. Everyone can daydream. You've probably been getting visual, meditative messages but mistook them for your own egoic thoughts. When they come out of the blue, unrelated to anything you were thinking about, that's a message.

Visuals often begin as mere flashes or snippets. Allow them to flow and express gratitude. If possible stop what you're doing and record them in as much detail as possible. Over time those flashes will expand. One day you may find they turn into virtual movies.

Don't try to control the visuals. Should a scene or object change shape, flow with it. Do not try to force it back to what it was. There's a reason it morphed. You want to move forward with the visual, not anchor it down. Meditation is all about flow and ease. That's why you feel relaxed and refreshed afterwards.

In this specific form of meditation where your intent is to connect with your Akashic Records and team, the information coming to you is of a Divine nature. That means it's encoded with the love, light, and *vital force energy* (VFE) of Creator. Each time you meditate in this way, you're topping off your energy tank with an infusion of VFE. Perhaps you now see why it's an important activity to incorporate into your daily life?

Once you become adept at connecting, you'll find it takes just seconds to form a solid connection, and mere minutes to receive a refreshing download of VFE.

You Can't Ask For Too Much

If an infusion of VFE were your only purpose, the experience would be complete. However, as long as you're connected, why not dialog with your team? Ask if there's a message or wisdom they wish to share at this time, or ask anything you like.

Don't be surprised if they deliver a message in the form of archetypes, symbols, and/or metaphors. Sometimes you'll get straight up answers. More often you'll receive answers that require some focus and thought to interpret. In fact, by delivering answers in this way your team is able to give you much more than a simple answer. They usually layer in deeper messages. You will glean what you're ready to receive, and at a later time when you revisit (you did write it down, yes?), you'll often discover another deeper message that was waiting for you to be ready.

I recommend Googling any symbols you receive. Approach your message like a big puzzle. It's your objective to find all the pieces and fit them together, which will reveal the greater message waiting there all along.

Lest you feel frustrated at a lack of straight-forward answers, understand this: your guides will not, cannot, tell you what to do. That is strictly verboten. They *can* drop bread crumbs, give hints, and deliver encoded messages. When you find or receive them, make a choice about what you want to do. Loving, gentle nudges are allowed, but telling never, for that would make you little more than a puppet.

I challenge you to accept *Metatron's 21-Day Meditation Challenge*. It will change your life in ways you cannot imagine, and friend, right now with the transformation humanity is undergoing, you need all the extra help you can get. Want to raise your vibrational frequency to access higher dimensional wisdom? Meditation will facilitate the process.

Meditation is the wisest investment in self you can make.

Akasha Unleashed Opening Prayer

Divine Creator, it is my intention
to open a clear channel to my Akashic Records
through which only truth and light will flow.

Help me to understand your teachings and to
incorporate them into my daily life experience.

Help me to put your wisdom into action
to create the abundance, happiness
and peace that I desire.
So shall it be for now until eternity.
Thank you, thank you, thank you.

Akasha Unleashed Closing Prayer

I thank the Masters, guides and
Teachers of the Akashic Records
For their assistance in my quest.

It is my intention to now return to
Third dimensional awareness.
Thank you. Thank you. Thank you.

Day 1

Metatron: Listen. Listen and learn. That which you desire is nigh unto you. Can you feel the energy drawing near? Can you feel the excitement building within your guide team?

True awakening. The fullness of awakening. A greater insight than you have had before. Greater perspective. Greater purpose. Greater potential. Greater risk and rewards.

Debbra: Really risk? Did that come from me or you?

Metatron: LOL it was you. Risk is nothing you need concern yourself with. It is not our practice nor intent to put you at risk. In fact when you are in alignment there is more risk in **not** doing than in doing. Risk in the respect of missing desired opportunities.

Debbra: (Hearing Hank Williams singing: *I'm So Lonesome I Could Cry*) "Hear that lonesome whippoorwill?"

Metatron: Loneliness is an illusion, for you always have your three selves (ego, higher self, soul), plus your entire team, who are perpetually bustling about on this errand or that in service of you. Allow yourself to feel them, perhaps even to see them. You may picture them in any shape, size or color you desire. Shape matters not to their mission and they will happily take on a shape and form that is pleasing, even delightful, to you. They enjoy your playful, curiosity-seeking energy.

Debbra: Note to self: stop editing, just record the details as they show up.

A noise outdoors is temporarily distracting. That's ok, I say to self. Wait until it passes. Take a couple deep breaths and go right back to focusing on your breathing.

Ok, where were we?

Metatron: No matter. We are here now. *Where* is the past.

What is next you wonder? Everything! More than you can possibly imagine in this moment. How much you actually experience depends entirely upon you. How much time will you allow for such pursuits and endeavors? That's the key.

Take meditation for instance. When you prioritize just 15 minutes a day, your spiritual growth will accelerate by leaps and bounds. Accelerate like a fine sports car. Accelerate like a puma on the scent of its prey.

Just as quickly as you accelerate, you may decelerate to enjoy each and every moment. Do you see the contrast?

Accelerate with mindfulness, so that you allow yourself the delicious experience of each juicy moment.

Debbra: My mind wanders… How much time do I have left?

Back to focusing on breathing. What's next? Is there more? Are we done?

Metatron: (Smiling at my impatience and speaking indulgently.) You know that anything worth having is worth waiting for.

Debbra: Pausing to check on pizza in the oven. Darn! Really screwed it up, forgot to take the plastic off the top.

Metatron: There is nothing so bad that it cannot be remedied in some manner.

Debbra: Breathe, relax, allow the messages to filter through. Ugh, I can smell the burning plastic. Will my pizza be ruined?

Metatron: It's ok. If it's ruined then it wasn't meant to be. There's always salad. Your fifteen minutes are up.

Debbra: But I can stay a little longer.

Metatron: No, for now stick to the plan. You will soon see there is a reason for it.

Debbra: Ok, thank you Metatron for your love and patience. Wait… what about my questions?

Metatron: They will keep. You have all the time in the world.

Debbra: Did you say that or was it me?

Metatron: It was you, there actually *is* a timeline and you need to be mindful of it.

Day 2

Debbra: Ok Metatron I'm here ready to take dictation.

Metatron: That is good. Let us proceed...

Today as we come together there is much turmoil in your world. Deservedly so.

Debbra: Deservedly? Is that the word you want to use?

Metatron: Yes, deservedly, it is karma pure and simple. The consequence and culmination of the gathering storms of angst, fear, hatred and bigotry. Those negative thought patterns have reached an apex, like a car radiator reaching maximum pressure. That pressure *must* be released. It must burst forth clearing some space for reconnoitering, regrouping, reevaluating priorities, assessing the consequences of actions taken whether consciously or unconsciously. This release must come as surely as the sun must rise.

While in the moment it may feel distressing, keep your wits about you. Have faith. Trust that you will come through the smoke and detritus of the explosive release. When the air clears you will still be standing. Standing firm in your trust that there is a higher power at work in the grand scheme.

Nothing is random.

You will soon enough see transformations beginning. Little by little, like-minded souls and you, yourself, will shift into a new way of being.

More accepting, more understanding, more loving. A higher vision of self and purpose. It is no accident that you are here at this time. There is a grand design, a framework from which you, through your choices, fill in the details.

The outcome was never in doubt. You always planned to come to this place of enlightenment and expansion. A time of peace, love, and great abundance. A respite from the days of fear and strife. Your soul oasis, somewhat like a soul vacation. (Big grin)

Debbra: That sounds lovely but what then?

Metatron: What then? Whatever you choose of course. In this new enlightened age you will set your sights higher. You'll have greater vision of what you might accomplish.

Many will work with Gaia to cleanse and repair, to nurture the land back to wholeness and good health.

For her part, Gaia will reveal new secrets heretofore hidden. She has been keeping them safe until the day of enlightenment. Working in partnership with her, humanity will be astonished at how rapidly progress will occur. Voices will be raised in delightful song — healing song.

Debbra: I'm almost hearing a frequency, but it's blocked. Metatron, were you going to share a specific frequency? I'm hearing 1021... gigahertz(?) megahertz? Not sure. My *doubt* about what's accurate blocks receiving the true number.

Metatron: Do not concern yourself with precise numbers. The most important thing is to see the big picture; to understand where you are headed so that you might put forth more effort to reach that pinnacle, leaving behind stormy seas for tranquil waters. Ride the gentle waves alongside the creatures of the sea. Harmony amongst the species.

Debbra: Does that mean we'll stop consuming animals?

Metatron: That is for you to decide. We make no judgment upon you in that regard.

Debbra: Thank you Metatron. Anything else?

Metatron: Namasté Dear One. Rest well and return once more tomorrow that we might continue our dialog. Blessings be upon you.

Day 3

Debbra: It's late. I hope I didn't wait too long. You still there Metatron? Uh oh, it's really quiet. The wind is howling outside. Wonder how much snow we have?

Just breathe, focus, you can do this. I just heard Alfred Hitchcock's voice say "*Good evening.*"

Oops, dry throat, need a drink. Too hot, can't focus. This is taking a really long time... Have to change position, maybe that will help. Darn, wish I'd remembered this earlier! (Meditating, that is.)

That's better. Long, slow breaths. Relax... Metatron are you there?

Metatron: *Always,* he whispers, almost like a purr.

Debbra: Let's get this show on the road.

Metatron: Patience, all in good time. Center yourself. Anchor into Earth because the energy is intermittent this night, at this time.

Debbra: Ok, grounded super duper well.

(In a vision) I see my younger self on a swing. Legs stretched forward, torso tilted back, long, brown hair flowing behind. Wearing a light blue shift with a yellow headband. Swinging on a massive oak tree — *white oak,* I hear interjected.

(Hearing singing) Sailing, sailing over the bounding main...

What does that have to do with swinging?

Metatron: Sailing, swinging, same difference. The energy is flowing and that's the point. Breathe, relax, and allow the energy to flow with freedom and ease. Allow it to carry you along its sinewy waves.

Debbra: Sinewy waves?

Metatron: Strands of electricity, yes. Flow with it like a will-o'-the-wisp without a care in the world, just flowing along like the tumbling tumbleweed.

Go wherever the wind guides you. Be wild and free instead of careful and stodgy. Recapture the carefree sense of adventure from your youth, before adult responsibilities took root upon your shoulders.

Debbra: Yes, that feels so much better, thank you Metatron.

Metatron: Of course. You simply need reminding once in a while. Rely upon your team to give you a gentle nudge whenever you become too heavily laden with cares and woes of the day. That is their honor and privilege.

Debbra: Like a gentle wake up call, I muse.

Metatron: That analogy fits.

Debbra: What's the correct nomenclature, I wonder? Stop trying to edit. Just take down the details.

Where was I or we? Tumbling along like the tumbling tumbleweed. Moving along... what's the next line? (From the song *Tumbling Tumbleweed* as performed by the Sons of the Pioneers)

Wow the wind is really howling out there. I need a hair cut, this hair is driving me nuts.

Breathe... focus... Cough, dry throat. Distractions galore... Sorry Metatron.

Metatron: (Metatron takes my hand to strengthen the connection.) Come let's walk.

We stroll along a hard dirt-packed, pebble-strewn road of sorts. Grass and trees frame the scene. The air is dry and still. Little puffs of dust poof up at our feet. It's warm so we walk towards a wooden bench, situated near a small stream.

As I look at the bench, a large shade tree appears over it. Way to go team! Taking care of all the creature comforts before I can even ask — or think of them for that matter.

Metatron and I sit quietly on the bench for a bit. Each keeping our own counsel it would seem. Or rather, it's the quiet energy of no hurry, just flow in the moment. Here I notice my thoughts are quieter. Less prone to flights of fancy.

Metatron: (Turns to look at me.) It's nice here isn't it?

Debbra: I nod yes.

Metatron: It would serve you well to spend more time in quiet introspection like this. There's far too much frenetic energy, rushing to and fro, deadlines, obligations, situations, too much fizz in your days.

Debbra: But Metatron, you've given me a big assignment and I'm feeling the responsibility of not letting you down, along with all the other commitments pending.

Metatron: (Nods in acknowledgement) Do you believe you will run out of time?

Debbra: Not exactly. I know I can slow time down. I guess I just drift too much into the fizz and momentarily forget.

Metatron: Yes. That's all right. Just make your course correction in the very moment you notice you've drifted out of harmonious alignment.

Debbra: Yes. More mindfulness is called for. As much as I share that with others, I still too often get caught up in the frenzy.

Metatron: Do not judge yourself so harshly you're doing exceptionally well.

Debbra: Really? I ask incredulously.

Metatron: Yes, you are. You've already come far and we are quite pleased. Just keep doing the best you can, making corrections, and don't forget to stop occasionally to appreciate your accomplishments. That is equally as important — as important if not more so — than the tasks themselves. Treat yourself kinder. More compassion. More appreciation. Be gentle with Debbra.

Debbra: (There's a feeling of near completion in my solar plexus.) Thank you Metatron. What else do you have to share with me today?

Metatron: We've already exceeded our allotted time. Let us take this up again tomorrow. For now it's enough. Wishing you peaceful slumber and a good tomorrow.

LIKE A SLOW MOTION PAN OUT OF THE CAMERA, I find myself back in present awareness. The scene and Metatron have vanished.

Day 4

Debbra: It's late again. This day was so crazy with shoveling snow and having to run to New Jersey to pickup David. Really testing my resolve to fit in a daily meditation. But, today I'd feel incomplete if I didn't, so that's progress!

Metatron: Breathe. Notice your chest filling with air. Now notice your belly filling with air. Remember to belly breathe. Really extend that diaphragm. Notice how relaxation follows right behind each deep breath?

Debbra: Yep. Is that enough? Are we ready to begin? I'm feeling very relaxed.

Metatron: Hold on, don't get so relaxed you fall asleep!

Debbra: That's why I'm sitting up... More deep breaths.

To self: Put aside all thoughts of what you were doing earlier and that endless to do list. This moment right now, connected to the 5th dimension is all there is. Focus. Relax.

Metatron: Ah, that's better. I've been waiting for you. Happy you could make it.

Debbra: Me too. I'm excited to hear part four. What's next?

Metatron: Today let's focus on stillness.

Bring your focus from outer to inner. Slowly bring your attention to your solar plexus. Allow your awareness to slip right into the very center of your solar plexus and rest there.

Debbra: Rest there? It's kind of noisy like a big factory, industrial sounding. Pistons firing, energy blasting in, around, and through. This is like an air terminal of an international airport. Is calm even a part of the vernacular in a place such as this?

Metatron: It can be if you choose to make it so. Keep your focus on the very center of your solar plexus and you'll notice the sounds slowly fading away until you see, or feel, yourself as a young girl, with fresh eyes and senses, enjoying the stillness and beauty of the energy as it gently caresses.

Go within and reconnect with that recently-formed human who's still new to this 3rd dimensional reality. Notice how she's centered, grounded, and focused in this space? This is her natural state now, before she is molded by people and events. She's content just to be, to soak up the lovely energy which fills her with peace and contentment.

Damn… hot flash! It's really hard to focus when it feels like my body is on fire. I want to chop off all my hair and strip or run outside in the snow and reset my inner thermometer. Right now it's stuck on 103 and I'm on fire.

Metatron can you do something about this hot flash so I can focus? I'd really appreciate it.

Metatron: Do not resist. That prolongs the flash. Flash means it should be over rapidly. When you resist it's as if you are doing battle with yourself, and you prolong the discomfort. Breath, relax, allow. That is the answer as with so many other challenges.

Debbra: Ah coolness is returning. That's better. So the little girl who's at peace, what about her?

Metatron: She exemplifies the principal of allowing. There is no resistance in her. She hasn't learned it yet. She simply flows and delights with each new discovery and experience. Notice the resulting peace and contentment? She is not consumed with stressing and striving. At her present level of understanding she would find it incongruent.

Debbra: Ok, got it. But is there anything else? I'm not connecting the dots here.

Metatron: (Chuckling) That is exactly the point. You are striving to peek over the top to find the answer. The answer is not without, it is within. Cast your gaze within and find your answers waiting there. Everything you need already exists in your seat of power, your solar plexus. The wisdom of the ages resides there. You need only tap in to find all the answers which you seek.

Debbra: So it's about introspection?

Metatron: Yes, it's your reset level. When you become disillusioned, overwhelmed, confused, frustrated, go within. Find your peaceful space. From there, observe and allow the answers to present themselves for your acceptance or rejection. Just because a concept is presented doesn't mean you must embrace it. You are free to choose the inspired thoughts that resonate with who, and where, you are at this time. Do not worry about missing out. Offers made will come around again at the next juncture point. Cycles my dear.

Debbra: So what you're saying is it once more comes around to faith and trust? Going to that place in faith and trust that the answers will be forthcoming?

Metatron: Exactly. It really is quite simple. There is no need to complicate things. Go forth and prosper, but first go inside to discover the inspired ideas which will facilitate your success.

Debbra: Wow, that's profound. Thank you Metatron. Anything else?

Metatron: Not at this time. Go in peace — not pieces. That's a joke.

Debbra: It's really not funny Metatron.

Metatron: Laughing, I guess you have to be on the other end of the stick to really appreciate that one. No matter. The lesson is still profoundly powerful. Reflect upon and consider until our next assignation.

Debbra: Thank you Metatron. #Gratitude.

Day 5

Debbra: Ok, here it is after 11pm and I'm just beginning — again! Why do I do this to myself?

Metatron: It's ok. You can go to bed afterwards. Focus, breathe, relax. That's it. Feel the tension slipping away. Keep coming back to your breathing.

Debbra: Wonder what exciting tidbits will come through tonight?

Metatron: Focus and you'll find out.

Debbra: Yes... back to that... A deep feeling of peace and contentment washes over me. Beautiful, delightful, exquisite. As if everything is all right in the entire world — even though it's not.

Metatron: That is an illusion. Everything is as it should be. There is a purpose and a reason for the current state of affairs.

It's a part of the metamorphosis, shedding the old to make way for the new.

Old thoughts, old beliefs, old patterns... release them all. Throw off any beliefs that do not feel joyous and expansive. You are the only one limiting your experience. Whether it be through fear, old patterns, lack of trust, or simply inertia, it's all within your means to control.

Debbra: (Ouch! Achy body from all that snow shoveling. Focus, focus..). You were saying about limitation?

Metatron: Just that... limitation. Why would you choose limitation when the Universe is at your disposal? There's nothing limiting about the Universe. In fact it's so expansive you may not know where to begin. We say, right in front of your nose. Start with that micro world, then gradually expand your circle of awareness, bit by bit, until you begin to understand what *limitless* feels like. There are no boundaries that you did not erect yourself.

You have freedom and space to expand your conscious awareness. Know that it will continue to expand as long as you remain inquisitive, curious, and move forward into expansion.

Of course you may choose to close the doors and windows at any point, however, we would encourage you to lean into expansion, for there you will find more of that which you are seeking. More love, light, peace, and joy. More excitement. More delicious experience. More knowing and understanding the truth of who you are, and what you came to accomplish. What you intended to *be* about.

As you come to this understanding, take an assessment. How are you doing? Have you made progress? If not, what's holding you back?

If yes, how does it feel? Are you ready for more? What blocks or obstacles have you encountered? How did you handle those challenges? Are you still hampered or have you found your way through or around?

Truly we say unto you: there are no obstacles you cannot conquer. You are so much more powerful and magnificent than you have yet to understand.

Big changes are on their way… Huge!

Embrace the opportunity. Revel in the expansion and feeling of accomplishment as you make your way forward to the next milestone. There have been many before and there are a great many more yet to come. Bask in the joy of your accomplishments and watch more opportunities present themselves for your experience. Allow joy, wonder, and delight to be your constant companions. This trio turns a humdrum existence into a wild and wonderful journey.

Do you remember what that feels like?

If you need an analogy, it would be like birthday and all your favorite holidays rolled into one. So delicious it might feel a bit decadent, and that's ok. That feeling is like manna from heaven. It nourishes your soul and provides the wind in your sails to carry you on to your next big adventure. Always more to be experienced, more delight to sustain you.

Debbra: The energy now shifts and I feel or hear a door close. Not quiet, not loud, just a firm confident close, as one segment ends and another begins. (What a funny way to describe it.)

Nevertheless this meditation has concluded. Time to wrap the conversation up and settle in for a good winter's night sleep.

Is there a sign off? It feels like there should be. I hear odd words, but not clearly enough to enunciate. Is that me trying to make up a word, or is that you sending words in a language I do not speak?

Metatron: Relax, don't force it. You can simply end. You don't need a fancy send off. However, if you insist we can simply knit in a formal *Selah*.

Good night and Selah.

Debbra: Thank you. That feels better.

Metatron: Mañana.

Day 6

Debbra: I skipped yesterday. Between a live event, writing my newsletter, editing video and shopping, I totally forgot.

Today I have a bad cold. Scratchy throat, runny nose, lots of sneezing, feeling raw. Scheduled Covid test for Tuesday just in case. Made chicken soup. After broth I felt better for about half an hour. Taking remedies, using throat lozenges, drinking a lot. Hoping to feel better tomorrow.

Onward... Damn! Every time I take a deep breath I feel like a sneeze is coming. Really hard to concentrate.

I'm here Metatron. Sorry about yesterday. This new habit hasn't solidified yet. Maybe I need to set an alarm.

Metatron: Ya think?

Debbra: I'm here. Plugged in and ready to receive your message.

Metatron: Yes, that is good. (Said in a gentle, deep voice.)

Debbra: A tentative deeper breath to see if sneezing ensues. Darn now a coughing jag.

Metatron: Slow and easy. You can do this. Take a throat lozenge. Breathe, focus, wait quietly. It's ok if it takes a little longer. Be patient. The message will come.

Debbra: Lozenge helped. May we begin today's transmission now?

Metatron: Certainly. We're always ready.

Debbra: (Waiting for the message) Well...

Guides: Don't be in such a rush. Anything done in haste is not likely to have lasting value.

Debbra: Fair enough.

Guides: La la la la la la la la la.

Debbra: Tuning up?

Guides: Sure if you say so. More like amusing ourselves while we wait for you to settle in.

Debbra: And maybe a gentle nudge too?

Guides: (Grin) You might say that. We have much to discuss and are glad of the opportunity to converse.

Debbra: Wow, that sounds like Esther Hicks' voice when she's channeling Abraham!

Is there any particular topic you have in mind for tonight?

Guides: The world is your oyster so get up and move it along. (Said in a sing/song way)

Debbra: I heard that song snippet earlier when I was channeling, but can't place it. Is that a message for me as well?

Guides: If you like. We're just reminding you in case you forgot. A little investigation is in order.

Debbra: Thank you for the reminder. I'll attend to it.

Guides: De nada

Debbra: (20 minutes in) I'm ready...

Metatron: Good, then let us begin in all earnestness. You come seeking a message. We have a message to share. What a marvelous state of affairs. Let's focus on untangling.

Debbra: There are so many topics I'd like to talk about. Is that the problem? They're waiting for me to choose?

Is that it Metatron? Shall I choose a topic.

Metatron: Of course you are always free to choose. What would you like to discuss.

Debbra: Can you tell me about the connection between the Star of Bethlehem and the North Star? (At the time of this meditation, December 2020, a rare celestial convergence of planets was imminent.)

Metatron: Yes, that is a good topic.

The Star of Bethlehem and the North Star are not the same star. They are decidedly distinct. The North Star is ever present and connected to Earth. That is enough without taking on additional duties.

The North Star is a guiding light. It represents stability, steadfast loyalty, consistency, reliability. It is eternal and fixed in its relationship to Earth.

The Star of Bethlehem, on the other hand, has a much larger orbit and comes infrequently. Its purpose is different. It is a herald star, heralding an event of some magnitude. Its size and scope are such that it cannot be overlooked. It incites burning curiosity in those who are more awake than the average person.

Those awakened ones will be compelled to study and analyze, research and probe, to understand this unusual appearance. They will be driven to understand the purpose and significance so that they might share that understanding with others. They are the ones who *connect the dots* for everyone else, so that they too might understand the significance of the event.

It has always been thus. Just as Joseph was chosen to interpret dreams for Pharaoh (Biblical Old Testament story), and be the catalyst that paved the way for the Israelites to return to their homeland; so too are these watchers part of something grander which is yet to be revealed. When the time is right, greater understanding will arrive. When the last dot is put into place it will all make sense.

Debbra: With this I get a visual of some sort of grand constellation coming together.

So the Star of Bethlehem is part of something larger. A cog? I don't understand why you can't explain it plainer than that so that I can understand and share with my followers. I promised I'd bring them more details. This feels wholly insignificant.

Metatron: You cannot see nor understand what has not yet arrived. For now it is enough to know the star is a herald. Why don't you do some research on herald?

Debbra: Are you saying there's some event ahead that will have the significance of Christ, but we're not yet ready for the details?

Metatron: Something like that. Yes it is profoundly significant. Everything will become clear in due time. For now, appreciate your interest and dedication. Allow events to unfold and reveal themselves in Divine timing. That is all.

Debbra: End of transmission (it felt like). Almost like a door closed. Given my runny nose and discomfort, this is more than I expected, so it will have to do until tomorrow.

Please Metatron can you send some healing energy my way so that we might make more progress tomorrow?

Metatron: (Said in a whisper) There is no hurry. Sayonara.

Day 7, Take Three

Debbra: No meditations the last two days. I showed up but my body kept me too distracted to meditate while battling a cold. Today I'm starting off fresh after a good sleep. Darn my keyboard is going wonky and I have a meeting shortly.

Oh Metatron, Metatron wherefore art thou Metatron?

So if I'm showing up and no message comes is this about me being disciplined and patient? Is it about waiting in that quiet space, trusting that when the time is right something will come?

Metatron: Now you're getting it. Easy to show up when messages flow. But not so much when they don't. Can you, will you, remain steadfast to your commitment even when it means sitting in silence with your own thoughts?

Debbra: That was unexpected.

Metatron: Stay sharp, stay fresh, lest you fall into complacency parroting what you think the message is rather than truly listening for the present message. It's far too easy to fall back upon what you already know than to wait in confidence and trust that new information is coming down the pipeline to you.

Debbra: My thoughts turn to an answer I recently channeled. I shared what I heard, but it felt incomplete, causing me to doubt whether what I said was true. With totally new information there's an uncertainty. Did I get it right?

Yet I feel there was truth there. Just not the entire picture. That's still waiting to be revealed. However, such new revelations take more consideration and time to channel through the busy thoughts that lie waiting to snuff them out.

Thank you. I can see why it's important that I schedule in a morning meditation, even though I'm not a morning person. It's important to show up ready, prepared to have a clear channel, not a sleepy one.

Metatron: Yes, and now go attend to your meeting attendees who will be arriving soon. We can resume at another time while you process what you have just learned.

Day 8

Debbra: My thoughts are all over the place today. Got my newsletter sent, now it's time to meditate. Working on the discipline of sitting quietly and waiting.

Thoughts come of John Denver, who was most decidedly a channel, and whom I just wrote about.

There's a headache forming at the back of my head.

The furnace kicked on reminding me how grateful I am for a fuel delivery today before the big storm.

I have no agenda, just waiting as quietly as I can for something to come through.

This exercise is about discipline, showing up, learning to be ok with silence, creating space for guidance to enter.

Metatron: It will do you a world of good physically and mentally.

Debbra: More thoughts of juggling family obligations. Noticing I'm able to focus on only breathing for longer moments of time.

Fragments of jumbled thoughts. Bits of conversations, movie snippets, flashing by like I'm floating in space, and they're floating past me.

Noticing but not engaging. That's progress!

Hot. Has it been 15 minutes yet?

Yes! Done for now. Feeling triumphant to have fit it in before midnight! Gratitude also for computer reminders.

Day 9

Debbra: Here I am, what do you have to share today?

I believe this discipline and silence is about something greater needing space to come through. Hard as it is, I'm committed to sit in silence for 15 minutes if that's what's required of me. A little challenging when my phone keeps dinging.

A VISION COMES: THE TOP OF MY HEAD OPENS UP and is flooded with the dark sky and stars of the cosmos.

Is that symbolic of opening up to more?

Tomorrow is filled with travel and family obligations. I'll do my best to meditate in the evening when I get home.

Vision continues: The sky and stars are pouring in through my open head. They're flooding my senses. Filling me up and pouring out my orifices. I'm overflowing with Universal understanding. Is that what's been waiting to come through?

A worry surfaces: how will I manage to organize, collate, sift through, and use that much data?

Vision concludes: File folders, neatly organized in boxes. All on their own, they collated and now stand ready for my research to begin.

EXCITING AND A WEE BIT OVERWHELMING, YET I wouldn't have been given the assignment if I wasn't capable of doing it. I can now methodically go through the data, compiling it into useful reports to share.

As the time is dwindling down this feels complete. One more day of successfully following the assigned protocol.

Thank you team!

Day 10

Debbra: Christmas. It was a great day. Food prepped, gifts ready. This year I chose what was best for me rather than accommodating everyone at my expense. It feels wonderful.

Late meditation, but feeling good and awake. Just a sticky spacebar slowing me down. Breathing, breathing, breathing.

I'm here. If you have a message, I'm ready.

Wonder who will speak today? Will anyone?

Belly breaths, expand belly on inhale. It's getting easier to sit in silence, except for coughing.

Thoughts racing ahead to how I will teach this technique. Thinking about a recent conversation on diving more deeply into the understanding and expression of soul gifts.

Thoughts stray to so many other tasks waiting for attention. Anything? Anything at all? Feels like a game of hide and seek.

Guides: Not a game. Purposeful exercise. Understanding and expansion will come.

Debbra: Will this process raise my vibrational frequency?

Guides: That could be one outcome. This process is multipurpose and far reaching. There are long-range benefits yet to be revealed. Results are dependent upon your dedication and determination to follow through.

Debbra: Thank you. That is reassuring. You know how ego needs validation.

Guides: Yes. You will discover there will be less need as your frequency rises.

Debbra: That is so good to hear. Sometimes that neediness feels like failure.

Guides: Ah, but remember how much more intense and pervasive it once was? Do not discount how very far you've already come. Remember the apex.*

Debbra: LOL, good point and analogy. Is there anything else before we wrap?

Guides: Com si com sa. Over and out.

Transmission ended.

* APEX IS A TERM USED IN EFT (HEALING MODALITY — tapping on energy meridians) to describe the curious

amnesia that sometimes occurs after a person, having been successfully treated, later discounts the treatment because they've forgotten how bad they felt before the treatment.

Day 11, Take Three

Debbra: Hello Metatron, I made it to Day 11. Filled with curiosity about what you have to share today.

Belly breathing. Focus... Hope I don't get interrupted, Francesca (granddaughter), is working on her reading assignment.

This chair is not a good choice for meditating. Darn, there go those FB alerts...

Distracted by thoughts of an upcoming podcast and what to talk about. Maybe by then I'll be ready to share about this meditation challenge...

I'm here, can the message begin so I can focus on it instead of bouncing around like a basketball?

Metatron: What do you want to discuss?

Debbra: Everything! Can you give more input on what to expect for 2021?

Metatron: Slow down. Don't rush. There are yet lessons to be gleaned from 2020. Be mindful. Find peace in quiet meditation. Look for opportunities to be peace and light for others.

Debbra: What about that weird dream that seemed to indicate my efforts were doomed to fail?

Metatron: No, that was not the message. Take your time. Follow the bread crumbs and ask for help. Know that everyone is ready. Do not fear those who would oppose. You are protected by angelic armor and *The Mantle of Light*. (A gift from the Akasha to facilitate my work.)

You light the way for others as it has been lit for you by those who have gone before. Yes, trust is a significant factor in this new state of your mission. We are forever at your side, holding you up, supporting, encouraging, whatever is needed will be made available.

Debbra: Thank you. I deeply appreciate all the support. Sometimes the mission feels overwhelming. Who am I to carry the Mantle of Light?

Metatron: Perhaps it would help to know you are not the only one?

Debbra: Yes, it does help. Less pressure to be perfect.

Metatron: You have been preparing for this over many lifetimes. We have faith and trust in you that you will not falter. It is a big responsibility for sure, but one which you are prepared to carry out.

Debbra: What about my family? Will they make it through the coming battle?

Metatron: Those who choose to remain will. This is not your concern. It is their soul journey to undertake. Focus on your own journey and allow each soul to do the same. Your role is to make the teachings available, not dictate how they are used.

Debbra: So in this lifetime I am a messenger?

Metatron: Yes that is an accurate description. As The Voice of the Akashic Records you bring our messages to the world.

Debbra: Is there more?

Metatron: Yes, but it will wait. Go and tend to Francesca.

Day 12

Debbra: Vivid dreams last night about discernment. Huge theme over a series of dreams: Discernment is a gift to yourself. Only choose the best, that which is aligned with your goals and dreams. This is the wise choice of an awakened soul.

Feeling satisfied at getting an early start today. Breathe, deep belly breaths...

Cinnamon comes to mind. Why? Is there a message to be heard? A lesson to be learned? Cinnamon... Breathe. If it's a message allow it to come.

Metatron: Plaaaayyy ball!

Debbra: Huh? Cannot settle in and get comfortable. My arms don't seem to fit anywhere. Lots of squirming around.

Yesterday yielded such a great message. Why isn't this getting easier?

Metatron: No judgment. Even if you simply spend 15 minutes with quieter thoughts it's a win. This is a gift to yourself. You can be even more the boss of your thoughts than heretofore. (Referencing previous message: *How To Be The Boss of Your Thoughts* see p 133)

Debbra: I'm noticing a small space of actual silence. That's progress!

Floating in a sea of nothingness. Soft and allowing. Feels like floating on a raft. Feet dangling in the water which is slightly cool. Allowing myself to be drawn in whichever direction leads to deeper understanding. This is an n=1 experiment. (A study involving one participant.)

Metatron: As it will be for each person who undertakes the challenge. No two journeys will be exactly the same.

Debbra: The scent of pine wafting through. Brushing against a soft long-needled fir tree. A feather drawn across my face over my eyes. Breathe...

So many questions percolating about the pine needles and feather. Contrast? What kind of feather? My eyes were closed so I didn't see. Breathe...

I see a burning piece of paper in front of me. As the flames spread and the paper slowly disintegrates, a dark pool of water becomes visible on the other side. Velvety, darkest blue.

Cough, cold, goosebumps as furnace blower kicks on but heat lags behind. Finally, warmth is replacing cold.

Metatron: Cycles. Life is a series of cycles. In, out, round about. Endless cycles. Like riding on a calliope. The brass ring keeps coming back around. As long as you're on the *ride of life* it will always come back around. There's an eternity of opportunities to take new action and create new results.

Unknown: Life's not done with you yet, a voice calls out.

Metatron: A metaphor: you sitting alone in a canoe without a paddle, seemingly at the mercy of the elements or fate. Yet, that's not true. For each choice you make propels your canoe. You are in control and always were. Helplessness is an illusion. All you need do is tune in and listen (like in a meditation), to connect with a list of options from which to choose.

Choose well and you glide through life with ease and joy. If that is not your reality, give yourself the gift of introspective time to connect with the desires of your soul. Once realized, make a new choice — rapidly — and observe how quickly your journey shifts into a more aligned state; which for you looks like gliding with ease and joy.

Be mindful how you *feel*. When the waters of your journey become rough and uncomfortable, make a new choice ASAP. Your canoe will course correct, bringing you back into the flow. When enacted with mindfulness and intention, you will soon notice that rough patches come far less often, and you are able to reset easier and faster. Being in the flow will soon become the rule rather than the exception.

Debbra: What about when the feeling of *stop the world I'm ready to get off* comes up?

Metatron: That would be the end of your journey in this lifetime, which propels you into a new, exciting journey.

No rush. Savor the journey for that's why you came. Soak up the lessons and have a great time delighting in the 3D experiences available to you.

Debbra: Ok, how does this connect to the previous messages?

Metatron: It will become clear when you have completed your assignment. Have patience. There are still many missing pieces to be filled into this puzzle.

Debbra: Distracted by thoughts of tasks waiting to be completed, the connection is broken. Today's session has ended. This time it was over 40 minutes.

Day 13, Take Two

Debbra: Missed yesterday. Today I'm preparing for a livestream. It's too hot. Feeling stressed, thoughts racing.

I need to get a channeled message before we start. No, not need, want, that's me being controlling.

Metatron: It can flow during the livestream as well as before.

Debbra: But Metatron it doesn't make compelling video when there are silences while I translate the words…

Ok, you're right. Trust! Breathe... Belly breaths. Plenty of time, no worries.

Metatron: Warmth, release, relax, breathe, allow the new energies of the future to caress and entice you forward into a place of happy anticipation of what you're even now creating.

Your pent-up desires from recent months are eagerly awaiting an opening to escape the dungeon where they've been trapped as you lived life in stasis. Nothing need have been postponed, merely modified, but we recognize when your hopes and dreams seem to be crumbling all around it is difficult to keep your head above water, let alone manifest that which you desire, and which was already in progress.

We invite you to take a big long exhale, releasing all those pent-up feelings and desires. Make space for new energy, new inspired ideas, and the excitement of bringing them to fruition. Whatever you can dream up you can create. Start with the small stuff and work your way up as your confidence increases. There's no rush — that would indicate an imbalance. Everything will come in divine, perfect timing and it will delight your senses.

Bushels of joy, wonder, and delight are all lined up ready for the moment you lean into faith, trust, and the excitement of your vision, then allow it to materialize.

Yes materialize. All that you have long desired is queued up waiting for you to open the door and receive. Breathe, relax, and allow that to be your reality. Your time is always now when YOU allow it to be thus.

Debbra: Distraction. The furnace is making weird noises.

Metatron: Declutter. Stop talking about it and take action. Words without action are just so much hot air.

Transmission ended.

Day 14

Debbra: It's late, very sleepy. Feeling a bit *off*.

Had a good day hanging out with Francesca, who lost a tooth and was eagerly anticipating the tooth fairy.

There's a bad, smokey odor outdoors that makes it hard to do deep breathing. Feeling resistance. Maybe I need to embrace and allow?

Deep belly breaths. Feeling some brain fog. Ascension symptom or Meniere's flare?

Would love to know what Metatron thinks of Doreen Virtue betraying their relationship?

Metatron: It's none of your business.

Debbra: Fair enough. Message received loud and clear: I can have all sorts of opinions about it, but none of them matter. It's her right to make whatever choices work for her, even though I and many others long for the days when she was the *angel lady*. I feel sad that she seems to be consumed with fear and loathing for who she used to be.

Ok, Metatron can you weigh in on my idea to make a video about John Denver being a channel?

I feel no resistance to my proposal. Guess it's time to do my research on John and make that video. I'm excitedly anticipating connecting with his energy. Such a fan girl (p 133).

Hearing John singing *I'd rather be in Colorado*.

Does that mean now?

John Denver: No, referencing the song, not the emotion it represented. That was then, this is now.

Debbra: Do you hang out with Jacques Cousteau?

John Denver: Of course we've had many fine conversations.

Debbra: Falling asleep, enough for this session. Tomorrow I'll get to it earlier.

Day 15

Debbra: I'm here Metatron. Can we revisit the conversation about John Denver?

Metatron: Of course

Debbra: Is it ok for me to access his Records?

Metatron: Why don't you ask him?

Debbra: Ok, I will. Wanted to check with you first.

That was easy. So what else are you ready to share with me about my new project: 21-day meditation challenge?

Metatron: Flow with it, allow your vision of the particulars to fall into place as you go. Those details are not important to nail down at this moment.

Debbra: You mentioned a fasting assignment. Are there any guidelines you'd like me to follow?

Metatron: Yes.

Debbra: That surprises me. Usually it's do it your way. Can you elaborate on the guidelines? Is it ok for me to start next Monday after I take Francesca home?

Metatron: That will suffice. Sooner would be better, but allowances can be made.

Debbra: What about length of time? What is the optimal target? (Big ba da boom drums sound.)

Metatron: Thirty days.

Debbra: All right. Is the optimal way liquids only? Tea and water? I feel yes in my body. So 30 days of liquid fasting it shall be.*

I welcome the opportunity to more finely tune my senses to receive more data faster.

Speaking of data, Metatron, can you tell me more about this research assignment? Am I to set up a regular data access/study routine, or am I to access as needed?

Metatron: Regular access would benefit you and others far more than sporadic studies. Setting aside regular time to study will accelerate your progress, which will ripple to others.

Debbra: Is there any particular direction my studies should follow?

Metatron: Your starseed work would be a good choice with which to begin.

Debbra: Ok, starseeds it will be. How long should I expect that line of study to last?

Metatron: It is never ending, however, you may expect it to require 2-3 weeks to gather sufficient data to teach as you have promised.

Debbra: Ok, sounds like a plan. Once I finish this book that's next on my list. Thank you Metatron. Anything else?

Metatron: No, this has been a fruitful conversation. Let us end here and resume on the morrow.

Debbra: Thank you.

* THE 30-DAY FAST IS SOMETHING METATRON ASKED of me. You need not fast. I only include it because it was part of my experience, which I have faithfully recorded for you.

Day 16

Debbra: Thinking about an access prayer and how to customize a new version that feels powerful, yet comfortable enough for anyone to use. Have a short time to meditate while Francesca finishes her virtual school.

Flashing on an odd dream this morning about multiple leaks in the roof of a house I was staying in. Ceiling was beginning to fall in. Lots of panic and stress. The weight of all the things left undone?

Come on focus. Metatron would you please share a message for the new year that I can turn into a blog post/video? What do you want to convey to the world right now?

A voice in the back of my head says the world is a pretty effed up mess.

Thank you Ms. Ego. Not now.

Allegorical story visions often happen during my regular meditations, and that is what happened next.

I've recorded this one exactly as it happened (interruptions and all), for illustrative purposes. As Metatron reminds me, this exercise is about expansion and helping *you* move beyond limiting beliefs.

This is but one example of how your angels and guides may choose to communicate. Being open, simply flowing with the experience (and recording it), is the best way to accelerate your ascension journey. They can also be fun!

Should your thoughts, or the outside world interrupt, focus on your breathing for a moment, then pick right back up where you left off. Your guides will assist. Just ask.

For now I encourage you to just follow the story to get a sense of what you might experience (audio link p 133).

VISION BEGINS:

> There's a golden, sparkling ball of light. As you gaze upon it, the light expands into a person-sized space, or larger. Certainly enough space for someone to appear inside if they choose to.
>
> Nope, no one inside, now the ball starts bouncing lightly up and down like a run-away beach ball, except it's moving in slow motion. Is it filled with helium?

The scene shifts to a sandy beach, with bright sunlight. Ocean waves gently lap the shore. For the moment, you're alone with the beach ball of light.

You take a few deep breaths, reveling in the exhilaration of the sea air. As you stretch and breathe, you become aware of the tight places in your body and begin releasing them one by one, with each exhale.

You're consciously communicating your desires while your body obeys. That causes a surge of power through your solar plexus. You notice, as if for the first time, how powerful your thoughts are.

You reach out and give the ball a few bounces, flexing your new empowered state of being.

The ball begins to slowly roll away from you, then back a bit, forward again. You suddenly understand that the ball is saying *follow me*. So you do.

There's a tingle of excitement and delight in following this beckoning ball of sparkling light.

Due to your excitement, you're not conscious of how far the ball, and you, have traveled; until you become aware that the terrain is changing. There are now black, craggy rocks along the shore and inlets of water that might lead to a cave.

Your pulse quickens as you hurry forward to see what you can see. The ball momentarily forgotten.

Sure enough you *do* find a cave. The entrance is somewhat small. It could easily have been overlooked if one were not on the hunt for it.

Once inside, however, the cave expands into a *great room,* punctuated by occasional salt sprays when the wind and waves line up just so.

Scattered thoughts of something and the word Mercedes. Was that a knock at the door?

VISION RESUMES:

The cave has a tall ceiling and appears to be quite deep. You realize, without light you're unable to explore. Just then your friend, sparkling light ball, rolls by with the energy of a beckoning *come on* finger.

You happily oblige.

Sparkling light ball wonderfully illuminates this space. There's a purple-hued glow in the recesses of the cave that's most intriguing, and you're anxious to discover the source of this glow.

Along the way, spots of red and white colored glow appear. Oddly, you discover they are man-made foot lights positioned behind smaller rocks along the wall. Is this someone's sacred space? Is it ok for you to be here?

A song plays: *You are a child of the Universe*... It's the chorus of *Desiderata (p 133)*, sounding as if it's being piped in.

As you near the deepest wall in the cave, from whence the purple hue emanates, you find a large flashlight in your hand, which you now point towards the ceiling.

A bat is caught in the spotlight, and as if in slow motion, flies down from the ceiling coming straight towards you. For a moment, fear creates a large lump in your throat. Then you remember this is a vision and you have control, so you lock your gaze on the bat and direct it over and past you. It's like your eyes are steering the bat. Pretty cool!

THE VISION IS INTERRUPTED BY A FEELING OF sleepiness. (After a brief interlude it resumes below.)

Debbra: What was the bat about Metatron? Why did the ball lead to that cave?

Metatron: It is the cavern of questions. This space represents your storehouse of knowledge. The bat is one of your assistants. When you *turned on the light,* bat was activated to serve. You may request bat to retrieve any information you require.

Debbra: That seems terribly inefficient. Why not use a computer, or better yet just visualize the data?

Metatron: You may certainly do that if you choose, however, there is merit in asking for assistance, besides it adds to the experience. More magical n'cest ce pas?

Debbra: LOL you have a point. What does this have to do with the 2021 message?

Metatron: Ah, I was getting to that.

Now that you have come to this state of awakening, you may consciously and intentionally mine the data of your Akashic Records. By you I mean everyone. It would be wise to focus some time and energy into practicing doing just that. The method of retrieval and visuals will be of your own making. Set the scene however you wish. A bit of attention diligently applied will reap large rewards, as a literal treasure trove of information awaits.

Past, present, future, details, karmic understanding, potentialities, connecting with loved one(s) who have passed. That and more at your fingertips. You have only to avail yourself of this resource. We urge you to grab this brass ring and make the most of it.

There is an uphill climb to come out of this dark period in your reality. We are your rock. Lean upon us. We will guide and inspire. Support and soothe. Delight and tantalize.

Be persistent and diligent in your efforts and soon you will find information and insights flowing with ease.

Flow and ease are your mile markers for 2021. Look for ways to *be* in flow and ease as you navigate the sometimes challenging terrain. Always choose the better, easier way. Be kind to yourself. Like a sponge, soak up all the wisdom freely presenting itself for your perusal. It is the time of expansion.

Vision concludes:

> A bright light (spotlight) shines upon you once more, obliterating the vision of the cave, bat, and everything that's not the spotlight.
>
> As you stand soaking up the warmth and energy of this light, realization flows through your being. You have just had a conversation with Divine. It was easy. It made sense. You are infused with a confidence that you really *can* do this and an excitement for more.

METATRON: THIS IS ENOUGH FOR NOW. RECORD your experience. Remember the precious details. Return to this energetic space and state often until you are as fluent in this language as you are in your mother tongue. Soon you will find that you are never more than a shift of consciousness away from accessing *all that is*.

This my darling, precious child is your birthright, always and forever. Use it to enhance your journey. Use it whenever you need guidance or even a boost of confidence. It remains available all day, every day. The 24/7 easy-access portal to your Akashic Records.

Debbra: (Ego inserts the theme from *Twilight Zone*). Ha ha. Not helpful ego.

Metatron: The vision is complete. Time to bring your consciousness back to present time and space. Take a couple of deep breaths and process the experience.

Debbra: Thank you Metatron, that was quite lovely and feels incredibly satisfying.

Day 17, Take Two

Debbra: Missed yesterday. Totally forgot because of the election drama in the United States.

What about the video on 45 and Putin? Is it a wise choice to make it? What other information is available to go along with what I have? I'm not at all sure about making political videos, even if the underlying story is about reincarnation (p 133).

My nose feels dry. Too many commitments. Feeling pulled into a million directions. I know I do this to myself by not putting me first. Today I am choosing to skip several Zoom meetings to focus on writing.

Lately I've noticed a feeling of jealousy that is so unlike me. It pops up randomly and I don't like it. What is *that* about?

So Metatron can you help me with this jealousy thing? I don't like it. Don't know why it shows up. I'd really like to cut the cord and be set free from it. I'm here. Ready whenever you are.

Metatron: (Chuckling) Well all right then. Let's see what we can do about these questions.

Debbra: Yes, please. Great, now I've got goosebumps to distract me.

Wow just realizing my 2021 is starting off as disjointed as 2020. I need to assert myself. Make some choices, take back control so I won't feel so overwhelmed. The heater kicked in, now the air feels too dry. OY! Where's my happy medium?

Sorry Metatron.

Metatron: Quite alright. My time is unlimited. I'm a champion multitasker with perfect focus upon each task simultaneously.

Debbra: Impressive! (Doing my best to breathe through the distraction of Francesca singing in the other room.) Feeling stress wash away.

Metatron: Shall we tackle the jealousy question first?

Debbra: Oh yes, that is weighing heavily upon me. It's like some big mystery waiting to be solved. Is it a past-life thing? or...

> Me, mine, more, more (I hear my voice saying). A feeling of being deprived, never having enough. Was that starvation? Neglect? Slavery?

I'm temporarily interrupted by Francesca, needing help with her computer.

Back to the conversation... Is it ego trying to compensate for soul asserting control?

No. A vision is revealed. It is, in fact, a past-life issue ready to be resolved.

Vision begins:

The incident occurred three past lives ago at the age of thirteen. It was a male incarnation and I was the oldest of 11 children.

My family was poor, struggling. I never felt there was room for me. Everyone's needs always seemed more important. I was the good boy who did what he was told and helped out with the younger children, as well as helping my father work the fields. There was little joy in my life and a whole lot of resentment.

A multitude of expectations placed upon me weighed a ton. It felt like being crushed. I longed to escape, but to what? There was no time to even allow my own dreams. Stifled, suffocated, trapped. Just wanting to escape.

By the time I reached 18, I was ready to leave and live my own life. My parents were happy to let me go, as the other children were now old enough to take my place.

Ouch! I had sacrificed everything, and yet could so easily be replaced? Resentment bubbled up. That's a sore spot — not being appreciated. Feeling jealousy that I had made such a small impact. They would move on without me, barely missing a beat.

In that state of mind, I had no understanding that my parents were giving me the precious gift of freedom. Totally got that wrong. They truly loved me and wished me happiness and success.

At that point all I felt was sullen, angry, and resentful.

Sadly those feelings did not dissipate after leaving the farm. Instead, I now viewed work through jaded eyes, measuring my value and self esteem by how others treated me. Especially important was whether they appreciated me.

Over time my work performance deteriorated, because I felt unappreciated. That led to being dismissed as I was no longer a valuable worker.

Bitter and resentful, I hit the road, letting my feet carry me to wherever, searching for a place, or people, who would treat me with respect and value me. The problem is, I was no longer someone who brought value to my work. The ensuing years were hard.

DEBBRA: OK I'M HEARING THAT I DIED AT AGE 26. That doesn't seem to fit with the story I just saw. Am I making all of this up? What's the scoop Metatron?

Metatron: Yes it's true. Your life felt like it had been long, but in actuality it was quite short. The remnants of that bitterness and resentment remain. You are free to release them, accepting how valuable you are. Feel it. Allow it to penetrate deep into your being, replacing old stories that no longer serve. Allow those stories to dissipate like condensation, leaving your heart and soul lighter and happier.

Debbra: Does this mean the jealousy will no longer torment me?

Metatron: It *can* mean that. You will need to intentionally release and replace those knee-jerk reactions. Create a new way of responding that feels better. More lightness of being is in order.

Debbra: That's for sure. Anything else? I've got an appointment starting soon.

Metatron: Go. Enjoy. Contemplate how you will shift these burdens so that you feel lighter, more motivated, and productive. The choice is all yours. All that's needed is new, inspired action.

Debbra: Amen, on that Metatron. Thank you so much!

Day 18

D**ebbra:** Missed the last 2 days of meditating. Too tired and too many obligations. Errands to run. Need to get my newsletter out and planning to make a video. First though, meditation.

Ok Metatron what shall we talk about today?

Hot, I'm too hot. Feeling a bit nauseated after taking magnesium. Ugh. Reminding myself the point of this exercise is to wait quietly. It's not about the message, it's developing discipline.

I let myself get sidetracked from meditating last night because of a stupid Facebook post. So much anger and outrage. Where's the joy of being alive on this great soul adventure? If you're angry all the time, you're doing this life thing wrong. Just stop it for your sake and those who love you.

Ok, enough of that tangent. Focus… Breathe, relax…

This was followed by a massive tangent on things that would make the world a better place. Darn those hamster wheel thoughts!

Metatron is there anything you have to share with me today? You feel distant.

Metatron: Today is not the day.

Debbra: Ok, is there some reason? You know my time is short today.

Metatron: This is not the time. Your 15 minutes have elapsed. You are free to conclude.

Debbra: Should I try again later?

Metatron: That's up to you.

Debbra: Ok, wrapping up now. Thank you Metatron.

Day 19

Debbra: Excited to get a message about the siege on the capitol (January 6, 2021). More info about DNA or whatever else is ready to be shared with me today.

Let the download begin...

Vision begins:

Tomato red is filling the screen before my eyes. Then fading. Streaks of yellow sunshine are now overlaid. Then it fades to a grayish hue that totally overtakes the screen.

Now changing to black and white, then mixed to mostly gray, but otherwise devoid of color, like the vitality of life drained away.

Waiting... getting really hot.

Just breathe through it. I hate that sweaty forehead, flushed face, hot back, hot-flash experience.

Now my upper lip is beaded with sweat as the heat floods my upper body. As I pause to fan myself, the color shifts to a dingy yellow/orange. Still waiting...

Trying to find a comfortable space to rest my fingers on the keyboard.

VISION RESUMES:

> The color is shifting again to yellow/white, with white being predominant. A black jot appears in the middle, just hanging there in space. Like an artifact in a document.
>
> Once I acknowledge the jot, it disappears. So it was seeking acknowledgement?
>
> Color now, more yellow than white, but mixed in a giant screen cover. In the center there's a hint of olive green. Like a booger, ewww!
>
> A hint of that green appears here and there across the visage, as if left by a gentle stroke of a paintbrush. Shading? But no shape is discernible. It's just random. Oh the randomness of the whole thing!

Is that the message? About randomness? Waiting...

> More white now. Is that because of the outside influence from the shifting sun? Or is it part of the vision? Maybe it's both?
>
> The guides just making use of environmental factors to assist? Yes, that feels right.
>
> Darker, more butterscotch yellow now flashing in. Then it spreads across my visual screen to become predominant.
>
> Layers… this feels like a message about layers. One layer combining with another to form a new palette. Then the whole thing is washed away by the next layer replacing it.
>
> There are colored flashes, reminiscent of aurora borealis.
>
> A sun-colored ball comes forward, expanding until it fills the screen. Then in a pulse, another ball comes.
>
> Sometimes the color starts at the edges, sometimes from the center. The balls are shifting, reflecting, and pulsating.

Now it's too cold. I'm getting goosebumps. Focus, breathe, stay in the moment.

> Slight gray shades appear, overlaid on the golden yellow. Are they eye floaters? Whatever they are, the guides will take the raw material available and incorporate it seamlessly. No need to worry that the message will be diluted or imperfect for it is always perfect. Sometimes the pieces just take longer to coalesce.

Only 2 more days left in the project. Shouldn't I be getting something more consequential?

Metatron: Do not judge, simply receive.

Debbra: Ok, focus, breathe, allow.

Metatron: Yes outside influences will always color the experience, however, they will not obscure as long as you are disciplined and allow the message to layer, to imprint itself upon whatever is already present. No need to worry. We will guide you to make sense of the whole picture.

Vision resumes:

> Cycling through light yellow to butterscotch colors, like rolling waves from outside towards inside and center.

Debbra: Ok, are you referencing the solar plexus chakra?

Metatron: Yes that is one aspect.

Debbra: Do you mean to say focus on the solar plexus during meditation?

Metatron: Yes sometimes that is the right answer, but not always. Be flexible. Check in with the solar plexus, allow the message to flow, then allow it to expand. When in doubt, return your attention to the solar plexus. Like a weak internet signal that pulses in and out, reconnecting to the solar plexus boosts the signal.

Debbra: Thank you, that's pretty cool. Is there anything else you have to share with me in this session?

VISION CONCLUDES:

> Silence, steady color, waiting... The black jot has appeared again. What does that mean? It's quickly gone again, followed by the olive brush stroke.

AH, REALIZATION DAWNS. NOW I SEE. IT'S LIKE WE took a voyage. This was the mooring place from which we launched, now we have returned to the launch point and mooring?

Metatron: Yes, the journey is complete.

Day 20

Debbra: Here I am day 20. What wisdom do you have to share with me tonight?

Breathe, focus... Song lyrics: *Butterflies are free to fly,* followed by *76 Trombones* (from The Music Man).

Why the movie soundtracks?

Metatron: Just random soundtracks to help you stay focused.

Debbra: Ok, except each song triggers related thoughts pulling me out of my meditation.

Metatron: That's ok, just go with the flow. See where the thoughts take you. They aren't random.

Debbra: *Music Man* is about a flimflam guy who fools a lot of people. There sure were a lot of devastated people in River City when they realized they'd been duped.

Metatron: And what did it take for those people to heal?

Debbra: It took seeing and/or feeling that justice had been done after Professor Hill apologized and prostrated himself. Even then some folks wanted more. They needed to see that he was really contrite and that a decent human being was inside the fast-talking suit.

For some that day might never arrive, but Hill put in considerable effort to make amends. It's all about making amends, which is karmic, right?

Metatron: Finding balance, yes. From a place of balance one can invite another to stand beside them on their raft and feel confident they won't fall off into the depths of the water.

Debbra: Ah, so it's about rebuilding trust.

Metatron: Yes, and being humble about it. Knowing that it will take the time it takes. It cannot be rushed or forced. Also it's important that the repentant tread lightly, making sure to stay on the straight and narrow lest they lose any speck of opportunity to regain trust.

It's about being steadfast and determined. Being consistent. Not giving up, and not slipping back into old habits lest much progress be lost.

Debbra: Ok, this is feeling like we've wandered way off course. What am I to learn from this? I'm not Professor Hill.

Metatron: Astute observance. Of course not. However, like it or not, people put their own expectations upon you, and you may not even be aware of them, let alone *what* they are.

When you shift, you may find you've disappointed them. They may feel let down regardless of whether they had any right to those expectations or not.

Now you have a dilemma. Mollify the one(s) who are disappointed, or stay true to self and allow them to fall away? Perhaps they were never your tribe to begin with?

You see it's far too easy to get caught up in what others want, and lose track of yourself and journey. We say you needn't bend to accommodate anyone, unless it pleases and/or serves you. Each person to their own.

Know that it is perfectly acceptable, and in fact preferred, that you tend to your own business (needs), and stop worrying about what anyone else thinks. Get into alignment with that which your soul craves and life will flow with more ease. You will be less perplexed about what people actually want and expect from you.

None of that is important. Remember it's all about you and your journey. There you have it. *The lesson is about not allowing the expectations of others to derail your plans.*

Remember butterflies are free to fly...

Debbra: Ah thank you for connecting the dots.

Yes, that feels better. Just like that person who left the rubbish review of my book (*Akasha Unleashed*). It's not my problem if he had unrealistic expectations.

Metatron: Neither is it worth being upset over. He clearly was having a bad time of it for whatever reason, and it's not your problem, so don't annex it and make it yours. Bless him and move on.

Que sera sera, what will be will be... and henceforth so shall it ever be.

Day 21

Debbra: I'm excited to conclude the 21-day assignment.

Breathe, focus... Feeling warm, filled with love and confidence on this completion day. Also very curious about the message. What will it be? Profound? Mundane? Both? Neither?

Metatron clears his throat to get my attention. LOL

Metatron: Shall we begin?

Debbra: Oh yes!

Metatron: Very well then, an auspicious occasion. Congratulations on hanging in to complete even through the challenges. Some days were better than others wouldn't you agree?

Debbra: Oh yes for sure. I'm working hard to stay out of judgment and doing my best to stay in the flow.

Metatron: That is good. It is all we can ask. Given the circumstances in your world and life, it is more than enough. We only need a small crack through which to connect. Of course, we prefer the times when you throw the doors wide so that we can bring in an entire marching band.

Debbra: Someone's in a humorous mood today. 😊

Metatron: Always. Humor is like manna from heaven. It will sustain you through hard times as well as good. Use it liberally because it is infectious and will positively impact those around you. Spread the laughter, joy and love.

Debbra: Amen!

Metatron: Crosses his arms over his chest, gives a deep sigh and gazes upon me. Seemingly deep in thought.

Debbra: I wait with bated breath.

Metatron: What shall we discuss today?

Debbra: I'm open to anything, you choose.

Metatron: Don't mind if I do. (He winks)

Come, he reaches out his hand and suddenly we are on bicycles pedaling alongside one another with a glorious sunset in front of us. Orange and red like the sky's on fire.

Debbra: Symbolic of Divine's heart afire with love for we, the creations?

Where are we going?

Metatron: Everywhere and nowhere. Remember it's not about the destination, it's about the journey. Stop wondering about the where and be present to enjoy the experience.

Debbra: Yes, you're right of course.

Ahhh, I lean my head back, take a big breath and feel the exhilaration of the fragrant breeze, along with the caress of that breeze upon my cheeks as we pedal onward.

The neighbor's barking dog is really distracting. Sounds like it's in distress. Maybe suffering from separation anxiety?

What if I send it some healing energy? Never thought of that before. Pausing to do so.

I sent an angel to stroke his head. He was quiet for about a minute then started up again. Sigh.

My message is important and I am not willing to spend more time trying to soothe him when I have no idea if it's possible.

Metatron: Not even for your own well being?

Debbra: Ok, can I hook him up to a cord that sends love and calming energy without my direct involvement and focus? I'm happy to help, especially if it brings me more peace, but I have a lot on my plate today and would prefer to get back to the message.

Metatron: What if the barking is the message?

Debbra: What do you mean?

Metatron: Reaches up above his head to pull down a spigot that looks like a fire hose which he attaches to his head. Then he opens the flow and lets it pour into the dog.

Debbra: Will that work? How long does it need to be attached? (I understand that Metatron is demonstrating a technique that I can use.)

Metatron: As long as it takes. Allow it to flow. You can monitor occasionally. Let him be filled to overflowing so that he is comforted.

Debbra: Waiting and watching him being filled. I'm feeling tension in my heart chakra. I need to relax and surrender to the task at hand. That's *my* resistance being called out.

Breathe through it. Don't let the barking distract. Focus, focus...

Now I'm distracted by thoughts of possible solutions. What if I volunteered to dog sit while they're at work. What would that be like?

No I really don't want to, but I *would* like him to stop barking. Can I find some compassion for his upsetment? Maybe that's what's lacking?

I don't know what he looks like, so it's hard to visualize and help. I'm seeing him as a pug. You'd think he would exhaust himself barking for so long.

This is not how I wanted to end my *21-day assignment*. Please tell me there's something of great value yet to come...

Metatron: You can always come back tomorrow for day 22 (said softly).

Debbra: Yes, of course I plan to continue, but I thought today would be extra special.

Metatron: Every day is extra special. That's what it means to be present and enjoy the moment rather than always longing for the next, more, better, day. Appreciate what you have in the here and now and it will expand. You will feel lighter, better, more confident, more at peace.

Debbra: Thank you Metatron. Ok puppy, receive the peace and calm of Divine that's even now flowing to you.

He's quiet!

Swing low, sweet chariot coming for to carry me home. That's the lullaby that comes up for him? Is he sick?

Barking resumes. In my meditative state I begin singing the lullaby. Darn, a headache is beginning at the back of my head... Relax, breathe.

Now I'm sending a ball of love and light to the puppy. It's orange/red like the sunset and floats over to him, touches his chest, then skips into his heart chakra.

...He's still barking.

A vision of baby ducks. Yellow with charcoal spots, waddling away quickly to keep up with mama. What are the ducks about?

Metatron: A sweet diversion from the barking. Intended to relax you. Who can be tense while admiring happy, little quackers. (Grin)

Debbra: A joke from Metatron. 😊

Now I'm singing *What's up puppy dog* inserting my own lyrics. Silence...

No! I spoke too soon... Is there more of our bicycle ride to the sunset Metatron?

Metatron: We can revisit another day. For now this is enough. I bid you adieu.

With that Metatron waves and vanishes. The 21-day assignment is complete.

Epilogue

Having completed my assignment, I spent the next month processing and seeking guidance on how to proceed. I knew my daily journal entries needed to become a guidebook, but how to structure it? What to include?

Honestly I wasn't crazy about the vulnerability of sharing my personal journey. Yet wasn't that the point? To lead by example? To teach what I've been taught?

So it was that on February 17, 2021, I went back to Metatron for further instruction.

Debbra: I'm here Metatron. I'd like to take some dictation for the 21-day meditation book please. Is there anything you'd like to add to what I have? I would deeply appreciate your point of view (POV) as would future readers.

Metatron: My POV is just make the commitment and put in the time. Remember you are building and toning a muscle. Some days you will be more distracted than others. However, it is important to consistently show up.

In time the dialog will flow like water. Refreshing, cleansing, purifying, enlightening. When you create the space and allow, the most marvelous insights, clarity and even positive change will happen.

Less worry, more follow through. Action is too often the missing ingredient in your endeavors. You tend to over think, which is where you get stuck spinning your wheels in the muck. Grab a friend and move forward together. Your meditations need not be solitary to be effective.

Find what works best for you then do it, and do it, and do it, until it becomes so ingrained that you will not feel the loss when you miss a day.

It always comes back around to this truth: if you won't put yourself first, neither will anyone else. Your needs are paramount to your success and happiness. Treat yourself like the most precious commodity — because you are.

Take care of self and role model this expansive way of being to others. In this way you will continuously create ripples in the pond that reverberate to the very core of the Earth. That is how powerful the simple act of self care can be when you consistently follow through.

In conclusion

Once you've completed 21 days of consistent meditative connection, I encourage you to continue a regular practice of connecting with your Akashic guides. They have volumes to share with you and eagerly await the opportunity to assist in your expansion. Truly in the small space of 15 minutes much *can* be accomplished. However, if you choose to devote more time to your studies, and expansion, that would further accelerate your spiritual journey. It's always your choice. We hope you choose *you*!

Where do you go from here?

- Keep asking questions
- Keep expecting answers
- Record those answers when they are received

This is how you build a solid foundation upon which to expand and flourish.

This is how you set yourself up for the very best life experience, which means your next incarnation will find you much further ahead as you begin accessing even higher dimensional storehouses of wisdom and information.

The wisdom of the ages awaits. You need only put in the time and effort to raise your vibrational frequency, which is the key that grants you access.

Debbra: Anything else on this topic Metatron?

Metatron: Keep it simple. Do not overcomplicate. This exercise is designed to be as easy as slipping on a warm overcoat. Comfortable, granting protection from the elements, a shield between you and the noisy energy of the great wide world.

Allow this energetic connection to be your safe harbor, your cocoon, where you will go on about the business of transformation into the new, improved version of you.

The peace, love, and serenity of a regular meditative practice is priceless and you deserve it. The only question is: will you give this gift to yourself? It's all up to you.

This practice is the very best investment of time you could ever make.

The gift you give yourself.

Afterword

My plan was to complete this book, publish fast, then launch a support group for the readers who would be led to make their own 21-Day commitment.

Metatron had other ideas.

You may have noticed he plays the long game, with every message building upon previous messages.

While I moved forward with editing and the myriad of tasks required to publish, Metatron triggered phase two!

Want some cheese with that whine?

In July I began getting strong nudges to launch the support group... NOW!

"But Metatron," I whined, "I'm not ready!"

There were so many reasons why it was bad timing, including (in my opinion), putting the cart before the horse, because the book wasn't yet published.

Ultimately I came around to seeing things Metatron's way (he's proved over and over again the wisdom of that). So I launched the book, and group, as a pre-release *beta*.

Almost immediately the brilliance of Metatron's plan was evident. The group launched July 11, 2021, and was rapidly populated with enthusiastic lightworkers, eager to connect with their own angels and guides — and connect they did. The results were beyond my wildest expectations!

Guard rails to the rescue

Because Metatron moved up the time table, I had no plan in place for how the challenge would unfold, other than: read the book, do your daily meditation, and share with the group.

That all changed when it became clear in the days leading up to kickoff that some sort of framework, or *guard rail,* was needed to navigate the challenge, and this new way of being.

So Metatron created guard rails in the form of daily messages. Sometimes they brought new insights, sometimes encouragement. Each one was carefully curated to meet individual needs.

As the days went by, people in the support group shared their frustrations and breakthroughs; while others reported astonishing growth.

Healings were reported.

Spontaneous connections with departed loved ones was happening for people who'd not previously had that ability Imagine effortlessly slipping into mediumship?!

The collective energy of the group was lifting everyone to new levels of potentiality, thus rapidly expanding their vibrational frequency — and facilitating their ascension.

From the broader perspective, more lightworkers preparing to fulfill the prophecy of Earthtopia. All the dots were marvelously connecting to Metatron's grander plan...

This is how you learn to channel with ease!

Channeling is something I've been wanting to teach for a very long time, but there are so many variables that the *how* proved elusive. Until now. See what I mean about grander plan?

And yet there's more!

Near the end of the beta 21-day challenge, I realized that the ending date was August 8, Lion's Gate... 8-8!

There are no coincidences.

Metatron planned everything — to the tiniest detail — to amplify your results. Even down to anticipating your enthusiasm and motivation to continue your meditation practice and expansion.

As day 21 approached, it was clear those daily messages were destined to become a workbook, which would guide and support future participants to successful completion of all 21 days — and beyond.

Earthtopia

Remember I said Metatron plays the long game? This challenge is first and foremost about *your* personal spiritual growth and ascension.

Then it's about setting you up to be in the very best position for what comes next — the ascension of Earth and humanity to fourth dimensional reality (Earthtopia).

Because you're reading this book, I know you have more than a passing interest in leaning into *your* purpose at this pivotal time of transformation.

Maybe you've been feeling the truth: that you chose to be here at this time, for the very reason of being a part of bringing the prophecy of Earthtopia to fruition.

Metatron designed this challenge so that you could effortlessly flow into hearing your angels and guides.

In the midst of a global pandemic, Metatron is throwing wide the doors for you to experience more confidence, more clarity, more faith, more trust in your team, i.e., your *personal* team who've been eagerly anticipating this opportunity to serve *you*.

Hang onto your hat baby, because life on Earth is careening into the time of the *great shift* — and so are you.

This is a consequential lifetime. You are living during consequential times. It's time to embrace the purpose you've been planning over many lifetimes with gusto and determination as you create your bright, new future and all that entails.

Abundant Blessings

Abundant blessings are my wish for you — because this body of work is all about *you,* beautiful soul.

Metatron is extending a helping hand so that you might unleash your potential and embody your soul purpose. Your Akashic team stands ready to assist 24/7, all you need do is ask. Remember: *you can't ask too much or too often.*

A Favor

If you found value in my book, would you consider writing a review on Amazon or GoodReads? It doesn't have to be long, all I ask is your honest opinion.

Your words may very well be the ones that resonate and help others find their own purposeful path. Together we're going to create some massive ripples in the pond. 🩶

Acknowledgments

A deeply heart-felt thank you to Sheila Olden, who's astonishing generosity planted the seeds of success for this book.

Special recognition to Wanda Resler, Rev. Mike Wanner, Melinda Van Fleet, Rev. Dr. Elena Skyhawk, Debbie Soderberg Kirchner, Dr. Donna Blevins, and Susan Brochin. Your role as birth doulas was invaluable.

To the adventurous, delightful, beta members of the inaugural meditation challenge, my gratitude to the nth degree. In signing on to Metatron's challenge, you embarked upon your own sacred journey of opening the channel to a deep connection with your own Akashic team.

Your commitment and dedication paved the way for those who will come after. The value of your contribution and support is immeasurable.

From my heart to yours, beautiful souls, thank you.

About the Author

Debbra Lupien, is a Spiritual Teacher, Author, and Voice of the Akashic Records.

She previously authored the international best-selling book, *Akasha Unleashed: The Missing Manual To You,* which has become a catalyst for personal transformation across the globe.

Debbra believes the holy grail of your soul journey is to find what feeds your soul — and DO IT. Wise souls avail themselves of the shortcut found in the Akashic Records.

In addition to writing, she regularly shares channeled messages, meditations, and spiritual lessons on her YouTube channel.

Connecting With Debbra

Debbra is available for private **readings**, **speaking** engagements, **workshops**, and live **channeled events**. Reach out to her through her website: AkashaUnleashed.com or via email: Answers@AkashaUnleashed.com

You'll find your **Reader Bonus + All Links** referenced throughout this book at: https://akashaunleashed.com/lightworkers-path

Also by Debbra Lupien

Akasha Unleashed: The Missing Manual to You

Co-Authored Books:

The Wellness Universe Guide to Complete Self-Care: 25 Tools for Stress Relief

Unscripted: How Women Thrive in Life, Business, and Relationships

Conscious Creators Magazine: Discover the Secrets of Awakened Women

Notes 1

Notes 2

Notes 3

Notes 4

Printed in Great Britain
by Amazon

79330754R00088